THE LAST YEARS OF LONDON'S RFs AND RTs SOUTH OF THE THAMES

MIKE RHOI

AMBERLEY

First published 2021

Amberley Publishing
The Hill, Stroud
Gloucestershire, GL5 4EP

www.amberley-books.com

ISBN 978 1 3981 0354 2 (print)
ISBN 978 1 3981 0355 9 (ebook)

British Library Cataloguing in Publication Data.
A catalogue record for this book is available from the British Library.

Origination by Amberley Publishing.
Printed in the UK.

Introduction

Many books have been written about these two iconic stalwarts of London Transport's history – and quite rightly so. The single-deck AEC Regal IV (Four) and the double-deck AEC Regent III (Three) played a principal part in the workings of London's route network for close on three decades, from the late 1940s through to the mid-1970s. This account, the first of two volumes, concentrates on their final years and the routes they operated to the south of the River Thames. The period covered is from around the beginning of 1976 through to the final demise of the RFs at the end of March 1979. At the start of this period the RT had all but been eliminated from central London with only routes 109, 155 and 176/176^{A} still scheduled to be operated by the type; the last of these succumbing in October of that year.

This is a personal account put together from the author's own collection of photographs taken over this period and supplemented by pictures taken by his associate of many years Dr Ian Derrick, who accompanied the author on a number of his trips to the metropolis.

The RT story began way back in 1938 when the Chiswick think-tank was charged with designing a new 'Standard' London bus. RT1 was the result which comprised an AEC-designed chassis powered by a 9.6-litre diesel engine and fitted with an in-house built 55-seat double-deck body. One of the innovative features of this bus was the sliding cab door which would remain a feature of London Transport's double-deck buses for the next thirty years. RT1 entered service from Putney's Chelverton Road garage on 17 June 1939. After initial testing and some modifications authorisation was given to build a further 150 of the type, which became Nos RT2–151. Mechanically these were similar to RT1 but the body, again built in-house, was of an integral construction. Whereas RT1 had received an all-metal body, the first production batch had bodies which incorporated wood-metal frames. They were 26 ft long x 14 ft 3½ ins high and were fitted with 56 seats (with one additional seat having been fitted on the upper deck). The majority of the batch had been placed in service by June 1940 but with the onslaught of the Second World War the last five trickled into service between March 1941 and February 1942.

Following the cessation of hostilities it was decided that with a few refinements the RT class should be built in large numbers. The major change in design was the reversion to an all-metal frame. While the chassis were again built by AEC the bodies were constructed by four separate body-builders – namely Park Royal, Weymann, Cravens and Saunders-Roe. One prominent feature of the early deliveries was the provision of a roof-mounted route number box which was later discontinued. History also deemed that the Weymann and Park Royal-constructed bodies were far superior to the other two, as these were eliminated from the fleet by as early as October 1957 (Cravens) and March 1971 (Saunders-Roe). As with the RT's successor, the Routemaster, a degree of swapping of body types took place when the buses passed through Aldenham Works for overhaul. The last major overhauls of the type were undertaken in 1970.

Construction of the RT bus eventually resumed in 1947 and continued without a break until 1954 when production finally came to an end. By then there was actually a surplus of buses and a number of the last batch of Weymann-bodied vehicles were initially put into store before being placed into service in the country area between 1955 and 1958. In all 4,674 post-war

Regents were built over an eight-year period, with around 870 initially joining the green-painted country fleet. Over the following years some buses were swopped between the country and central areas and vice versa. At the same time buses of a similar design but mounted on Leyland chassis, designated as the RTL and RTW, were also being constructed but the last of these were withdrawn by the end of 1970 and are not part of this story.

At the beginning of the 1970s there was still in excess of 3,300 RTs in service, and together with the RMs they dominated the central area routes but, with the implementation of 'OPO' and the introduction of Daimler Fleetlines and AEC Merlins and Swifts in some numbers, under the LT Reshaping Plan, this figure had dropped dramatically by January 1976. The remaining routes throughout the network scheduled for RT operation on Mondays to Fridays required 640 buses, with 365 of these being allocated to twelve garages in the south to work twenty different routes (with involvement with a further three routes on Saturday/Sunday). These were distributed as follows (conversion dates in parenthesis):

A	Sutton	43	93 (25/3/76), 164 (16/1/77), 164A (16/1/77)
AC*	Willesden		176 (11/3/76)
AL	Merton	15	155 (9/1/77)
AM	Plumstead	33	122 (22/4/78)
AW	Abbey Wood	15	161A (21/5/77)
BN	Brixton	30	109 (23/5/76), 118 (SuO) (23/5/76)
BX	Bexleyheath	33	89 (22/4/78), 229 (21/5/77)
K	Kingston	14	71 (4/3/78)
SP	Sidcup	58	51 (13/6/76), 51A (21/5/77), 161 (21/5/77), 228 (21/5/77), 229 (21/5/77)
TB	Bromley	25	94 (28/8/78), 119 (2/5/76), 119A (2/5/76), 146 (22/4/78)
TH	Thornton Heath	32	109 (3/10/76), 130 (SuO) (3/10/76)
TL	Catford	55	54 (22/4/78), 75 (26/2/77), 94 (28/8/78)
WL	Walworth	12	176 (21/3/76), 176A (21/3/76)

* Northern Area Garage

The highest concentrations of the type could therefore be seen in Kingston in the west, Brixton, Croydon, Wimbledon and Sutton in the south and Bexleyheath, Bromley, Catford, Lewisham, Sidcup and Woolwich in the east. Sidcup had the largest allocation for five routes closely followed by Catford, which catered for three routes. The largest single allocation of buses to one route was the thirty-three scheduled from Plumstead garage for the 122 although the combined total for the 109 was for sixty-two RTs from two garages. Of special note was the 146 worked by Bromley garage, which served a rural landscape contained within an urban conurbation. Three significant dates in the elimination of RTs in the south were 21 May 1977 when the remainder of Sidcup's allocation was wiped out in one fell swoop, 22 April 1978 when routes 54, 89, 122 and 146 were all converted to alternative types on the same day and Saturday 26 August 1978 when RTs ran for the last time in the southern area on route 94; this eliminated the remaining examples of the type from Bromley and Catford garages leaving just routes 62 and 87 at Barking.

Records show that there were just forty-four green examples still licensed for service at the start of the period under review, of which sixteen were based in the north and the remainder in the south. Of these seventeen were based and Chelsham, seven at Leatherhead, two at Reigate and one each at Godstone and East Grinstead. The Chelsham allocation was mainly employed on route 403 and they were also known to make appearances on the 453. Buses on the former route could still be seen on a regular basis at Croydon well into 1977. Leatherhead used their allocation of RTs on the 406 and these worked into Kingston on a regular basis until the last of the type was withdrawn from that garage in March 1977; the two Reigate-based Regents could also be seen on the 406. Two of Chelsham's RTs lasted into 1978 with RT1018 being withdrawn in May and RT604 continuing in service through to September; both of these Regents had received NBC leaf-green livery.

As the 1950s took hold and the new family of RTs began to settle down on the central area routes the design team turned their attention to producing a standard single-deck type which could be used on some of the outlying central area routes, but more particularly in the country area and on the expanding Green Line network of cross-city routes. With the chassis again built by AEC and based on the Regal IV marque, the initial twenty-five buses (RF1–25) were fitted with 35-seat Metro-Cammell-built bodies and designated as private hire buses. They were first allocated to seven central garages between April and June 1951. The whole batch was later refurbished for use on Green Line services. The next 263 buses (RF26–288), which were fitted with 39-seat bodies (with the length having been extended from 27½ to 30 ft), were allocated from new to the Green Line services over a twelve-month period from October 1951. Next to benefit were some of the central area routes with the introduction of a further 225 vehicles (RF289–513) painted in central area red; these were fitted out with forty-one seats but did not have doors, at the insistence of the Metropolitan Police. The final 187 machines (RF514–700) of this 700-strong class were allocated to country area garages with the last entering service in December 1953. Over the ensuing years a certain amount of renumbering and transfer of buses between divisions took place. Additionally the central area buses were later fitted with doors and equipped for 'OPO'. Of the 137 red RFs scheduled for service on Monday to Friday, at the start of 1976, eighty-five were required in the south. These were distributed as follows (conversion dates in parenthesis):

A	Sutton	12	80 (27/6/76), 80^A (27/6/76)
AV	Hounslow	15	202 (17/4/77), 237 (17/4/77)
FW	Fulwell	13	206 (22/8/76), 264 (18/7/76)
K	Kingston	34	71 (SuO) (26/9/76), 201 (7/11/76), 216 (26/9/76), 218 (31/3/79), 219 (31/3/79)
N	Norbiton	5	201 (7/11/76), 215 (7/11/76)
TC	Croydon	6	234^A (30/1/77)

By far the greatest requirement was at Kingston where, along with nearby Norbiton, thirty-nine buses were required for five services. The normally RT-operated 71 was worked by just three RFs on a Sunday, on which day of the week the route only ran between Kingston and Richmond. By the end of April 1977 only the 218 and 219 remained RF-worked, a situation which prevailed for almost another two years. In order to cope with the need to keep the RFs going London Transport took the somewhat unusual step of recertifying twenty-five of the type in 1977/8 with the work being undertaken at Stonebridge Park and Hanwell garages.

Meanwhile of the combined Green Line and country area buses only around seventy survived in service until 1976. These were used on a variety of routes from a number of garages throughout the London Country operating area, usually deputising for more modern types. The last original country RF to be withdrawn was RF684 at Chelsham in May 1978, the only one of the type to remain in use after September 1977, while the last two former Green Line examples were RF221 at Chelsham and RF202 at Northfleet, which were withdrawn in March and July 1979 respectively.

In the main the pictures featured in this account were taken using a Kodak Pocket Instamatic 60 camera which was fitted with a F2.7 26 mm Ektar lens. Shutter speed varied from 10 seconds to 1/250th of a second with a focal range of 3 ft to infinity. The camera was designed for use with Kodakcolor or Kodachrome 110 cartridge film, which produced 16 mm negatives or transparencies. With the advance of scanners it has been possible to scan the original negatives and transparencies using an Epson Perfection V700 scanner. The scans of these forty-year-old originals were cleaned up and the colours restored using the Photoshop Elements 9 programme. It must be appreciated that with the small size of the original negatives, some of the pictures may have lost a little clarity when enlarged, although the lens fitted to the camera was deemed to be of excellent quality for the type of camera when it was first introduced in 1972. Photographs provided by Dr Derrick were taken using an Olympus Trip camera which was fitted with a 40 mm F2 lens with a maximum shutter speed of 1/200th of a second, using 35 mm Kodachrome transparency film and are denoted as thus - (ID).

The author would like to acknowledge reference to the websites maintained by Ian Armstrong and Ian Smith with regards to the vehicle requirements for London bus routes and information relating to London Transport buses and to the RED-RF website maintained by Peter Osborn.

Books consulted include:

Blacker, Ken, *RT: The Story of a London Bus* (London: Capital Transport Publishing, 1979).
Joyce, J., *London Transport Bus Garages since 1948* (London: Ian Alan Ltd, 1988).

The following abbreviations have been used a number of times throughout the book:

AEC-Associated Equipment Company, LGOC-London General Omnibus Company, LCBS-London Country Bus Services, LT-London Transport, NBC-National Bus Company, 'OPO'-One Person Operated, PH-Public House, PSV-Passenger Service Vehicle.

Mike Rhodes
December 2020

AW Abbey Wood

When RT196 was photographed passing Chislehurst War Memorial in Centre Common Road, on 7 October 1976, it was the second lowest numbered Regent still in service, after RT192. Abbey Wood garage was responsible for providing the buses for the 161^{A}. RT196 was withdrawn two months later but was fortunately saved for preservation.

Services 161 and 161^{A} followed the same route as far as Chislehurst, where the former terminated with the 161^{A} continuing on to Petts Wood Station. Fifteen buses were required to operate the route on Monday–Friday. Abbey Wood garage's RT2156 is seen in Station Square at Petts Wood Station on the same date as the above. This bus stand no longer exists having been replaced by a taxi stand.

A number of 161^{A} duties terminated at Chislehurst War Memorial with the bus stand situated on its own short section of road in Royal Parade. RT2345 was captured after dark on Friday 28 January 1977. The crew had kindly left the internal lights on for the benefit of the photographer.

Seen in the daylight in exactly the same location three days later is RT2758. This was another 161^{A} duty that terminated short of the final destination. The 161^{A} had first been introduced on 6 May 1953, running between Petts Wood and Greenwich with RTLs; these were replaced by RTs in May 1955.

Also on 31 January 1977 RT2853 is seen in Chislehurst High Street, passing the common and heading for Petts Wood. Abbey Wood lost its RTs in May when Routemasters took over and RT2856 was transferred to Bromley but only managed a couple of months of service there before being disposed of.

RT2742 is followed into the Royal Parade terminus by RT4712 on 9 April 1977. The latter is on the 161, which was worked separately during the week by Sidcup garage. At this time the Sunday allocation was split between the two garages using Routemasters. However RTs were ousted from both routes on 21 May when RMs took over completely.

BX Bexleyheath

No mistaking where this picture was taken. RT696 is laying over on the garage forecourt on 7 July 1976. Besides being solely responsible for the allocation of buses on the 89, Bexleyheath shared the allocation of Regents on the 229 with Sidcup. Bexleyheath garage was built to house trolleybuses and opened on 10 November 1935. Route 89 received an allocation of RTs as early as October 1948, with routes 96, 132 and 229 following by 1959 (ID).

Eltham Well Hall Bus Station is depicted on 4 June 1977 with RT822 on the 89, DMS1602 on the 126 and DMS1411 on the 61. The 89 ran from Lewisham to Eltham Well Hall by way of Bexleyheath, thereby performing an elongated u-shape route. This bus station was replaced by a new one in March 1985 (on the opposite side of Well Hall Road) that was built above a new underpass for the A2 trunk road.

Blackheath Common was still criss-crossed by three RT-operated routes in 1977, the 54, 75 and 89. Monday 6 June 1977 was a day of heavy showers and bursts of sunshine in the capital. RT2501, which had been a country area bus until November 1965, is illuminated by the sun as it passes along the soaking wet road surface of Prince of Wales Road.

RT422 was photographed on the 89 in Lewisham High Street earlier in the day, before the weather turned really nasty. It is just setting out on its convoluted journey to Eltham. On the opposite side of the road, in front of the bus, MacFisheries had become the Money Shop and Dixons was M. M. Quality Halal Meats by 2019.

Bexleyheath turned out just four RTs for the 89 on a Sunday, as opposed to nineteen during the week. RT1932 is seen in Erith Road, opposite the garage, on Sunday 30 January 1977. This particular Regent was sold out of service later in the year.

RT2484 was new in January 1950 and was fitted with a Weymann body. After more than two decades moving around the LT network it finally settled at Bexleyheath in October 1975. In this view it has stopped at the Academy Road bus stop in Shooters Hill Road. Adjacent is the Greenwich Free School; given the name Victoria House when it opened in 1909, it was originally the living quarters for the Royal Army Medical Corps, until it was sold as recently as 2013.

For many years buses that terminated in the centre of Lewisham did so in either Molesworth Street or Rennell Street, alongside the old Gaumont Palace Theatre, which was opened on 12 December 1932. In 1962 it passed to the Odeon Group and survived until 1991 when it was demolished to accommodate road improvement works. RT2182 is pictured resting in Rennell Street on 10 March 1978.

The last day of RT-operation on the 89 was 21 April 1978 and thereafter Bexleyheath garage was devoid of Regents (other than Trainers). RT2484 is seen passing the entrance to Blackheath Station on the last day. The School of Motoring is no more but the station entrance has been sympathetically restored. The Railway hostelry is still serving pints and Double Diamond, brewed in Burton-upon-Trent since 1876, is still sold as a keg beer.

Above and below: Two last day pictures of Regents on the 89 sees RT2484 again (above) turning from Eltham High Street into Well Hall Road and RT4712 (below) in Bexleyheath Broadway. In the upper view the building on the left is now a McDonalds Restaurant while in the lower vista this section of the Broadway has been pedestrianised. The clock, situated at the junction of Market Place, is showing 13.20. Additionally all the buildings on the right have been demolished and replaced by the Broadway Shopping Centre, which was opened in March 1984. Meanwhile the fate of the two Regents couldn't have been more different; while RT2484 was resting in a Yorkshire scrapyard just two months later, RT4712 has since enjoyed an active existence in preservation.

Above and below: Bexleyheath also contributed fourteen buses to the twenty-three bus allocation for service 229 with Sidcup providing the balance. RT2743 (above) is seen at the southern terminus, alongside Orpington Station, on 7 October 1976 while RT1282 (below) was photographed at the Hare Street stand in Woolwich on 9 April 1977. At Orpington Station the bus stops are now outside the station entrance while Hare Street no longer plays host to any bus stands. Keeping RT1282 company is Sidcup's RT1586 on the 161 to Chislehurst. The late lamented Wimpy Bar is now part of the Starr Banqueting establishment. The 229 was replaced by a new route numbered 269 six weeks later.

Bexleyheath retained a number of RTs after the 89 was converted to RM-operation for Driver Training duties. RT3310 is seen climbing Knights Hill in West Norwood on 21 July 1978. An RM can be seen at the entrance to Norwood garage; this garage closed in 1981 and was replaced by a new structure on the same site, which opened in 1984. Advertisements for beer and cigarettes are no longer found on public advert hoardings.

TB Bromley

The long 47 route, operated by Dalston, Bromley and Catford garages, continued to see more than the occasional appearance by Regents from the latter two garages, long after the route had been converted to Routemaster operation in January 1975. Bromley's RT2804 was photographed in its home town's High Street on 1 June 1977. This section of the High Street has since been pedestrianised and the Boots store has gone.

The on-street parking of buses in Lewisham came to an end on 22 April 1978 when a new bus station (since demolished to make way for redevelopment) was opened. Another of Bromley's Regents, former country bus RT4190, was showing a blind for the Farnborough destination on 25 August 1978. Daimler Fleetline DMS2351 can also be seen on the now 'OPO' 89.

On 1 June 1977 the opportunity presented itself for the photographer to take a ride on an RT to the Farnborough terminus of the 47. However having boarded RT3750 in Bromley the Regent failed with mechanical problems after advancing no further than Bromley garage. The errant bus is seen outside the garage with an RM and DMS in tow.

In 1976 Bromley still had an allocation of Regents that were scheduled for routes 94 and 146. Additionally and almost on a daily basis the type also turned up on the 47 and 119. RT397 is seen on 3 September 1977 heading south along Tweedy Road, close to Bromley North Station. The street view behind the bus has since changed dramatically.

RT2804 was photographed wending its way down Bromley High Street on 21 January 1978. Bromley Common was an alternative nomenclature for Bromley garage. It is passing the junction of Elmfield Road. Bromley has benefitted from a significant amount of redevelopment work since this picture was taken and a new building, which forms an entrance to the Glades Shopping Centre, now occupies the site of Dolcis shoe shop.

Bromley again and RT379 is negotiating the Market Square on the penultimate day of RT-operation on the 94, 25 August 1978; this also being the last scheduled route operated by Regents south of the Thames. On Monday–Friday the 94 ran from Lewisham to Orpington via Petts Wood and was worked by Bromley and Catford garages. Amazingly RT379's inevitable fate was delayed as it was moved to the last outpost at Barking, for further service. Lloyds Bank now occupies the Caters Fresh Food Emporium. Along with RT Nos 394 and 557, RT379 was one of the last of the type to be overhauled at Aldenham Works.

Later the same day RT2143 was captured opposite The Fairway in Southborough Lane at Petts Wood on a southbound journey. Indications that it must have been a warm day are the open cab door (health & safety would suffer apoplexy now) and the dropped upper deck window.

RT1790, which moved on to Barking, has terminated at Petts Wood Station for the journey back to Lewisham. The 161^{A} terminus was just the other side of the railway footbridge. This scene is largely unchanged except the concrete road has been overlaid with tarmac and the post box is no longer there.

RT1850 was another escapee from Harrow Weald having been ousted from the 140 in July 1978. Seen in Orpington High Street, near the junction of Church Hill, its time in service at Bromley only lasted a matter of weeks as it assumed Driver Training duties shortly after this picture was taken. This view is largely unchanged although Barclays Bank (behind the bus) is now Pizza Express.

RT1850 is seen again on the penultimate day. Now having travelled further north it was photographed in College Road (with the junction of Paxton Road) at Sundridge Park (just north of Bromley). A medical centre has since been built on the site of the advertising hoardings.

During Saturday shopping hours the 94 was extended at its northern end from Lewisham to Brockley Rise. RT3220 stands at the Brockley Rise terminus (at the junction of Stondon Park) on the very last day, Saturday 26 August 1978. The petrol filling station has since been demoted to a car wash and MOT centre.

The 119, which was a fairly short route and ran between Bromley North Station and West Croydon, was exclusively worked by Bromley garage. Having been converted to Routemaster operation on 2 May 1976, Bromley continued to roster the occasional Regent, as demonstrated by RT785, which was photographed in Wellesley Road in Croydon on 1 June 1977. A borrowed Maidstone Atlantean is following on London Country service 403. The London Tramway now sweeps round from the right.

RTs continued to make appearances on the 119 to the very end. While Catford's RT651 was still normal fayre on the 94, Bromley had turned out RT1599 on the 119 on the penultimate day of RT working in the south, 25 August 1978. The pair are seen in Bromley High Street, close to the junction of Ravensbourne Road. The Debenhams store is now occupied by Dreams and Wilkos.

RT1599 was captured again on the 119 on the same day, this time in Wickham Road at Shirley. It has paused outside the Baptist Church, although the waiting lady passenger seems to be totally disinterested; she is possibly waiting for a mundane Fleetline on the 166 or 194.

Bromley garage's other regular RT-operated route was the 146. This was more of a country-style route encapsulated in an urban bubble. Running from Bromley North to the village of Downe, the last part of the route is through unspoiled countryside. Only a basic hourly service was provided over the full length of the route and RT2821 is seen at journey's end on 7 October 1976.

On a warm summer day in June 1977 RT3202 was recorded in Baston Road, alongside Hayes Common. Only three buses were required to operate the service on Monday–Friday, with two on Saturdays and a single bus (by then scheduled for a Routemaster) on a Sunday. First introduced as a mainly Sundays-only route (in conjunction with the 146^{A}) it originally ran from Lewisham to Westerham Hill. The route was suspended for the full duration of the Second World War and also during the winter months in the preceding and following years. Having subsumed the 146^{A} in May 1952 it became a daily route between Bromley and Downe with operation by RTs from Bromley garage.

On the same day RT1560 has worked a short journey to Keston (Fox) and is seen on the stand in Commonside. The original Fox Inn was most likely established in the early nineteenth century whereas the present, much bigger structure has the appearance of a pre-Second World War incarnation.

Above and below: RT785 waits at the village stand at 07.10 for the first departure of the day from Downe to Bromley, on 3 September 1977. The stand is adjacent to St Mary's Church, which dates from the mid-nineteenth century and is a Grade II listed building. Down House, the former home of Charles Darwin (and his family) from 1842 until his death in 1882, is situated about a quarter of a mile along Luxted Road, which disappears off to the right in the lower picture. The house is now open to the general public. Several members of Darwin's extended family are buried in the church yard.

The Bromley stand for the 146 was (and still is) in Tweedy Road, at the front of Bromley North Station. RT3778 is just arriving back from its trip to the countryside on 3 September 1977 and is seen passing London Country Northern Counties-bodied Daimler Fleetline AF1. Tweedy Road is now a wider thoroughfare and has since benefitted from substantial redevelopment work.

Another of Bromley's trusted steeds; RT1892 was photographed in Bromley High Street on 21 January 1978 in the early stages of its five-mile trip to Downe. The upper section of the High Street (north of Elmfield Road, which is on the right) has since been pedestrianised. Dunn & Co. is another well-known high street name from the 1970s that is no more.

Above and below: The last day of RT-operation on the 146 was Friday 21 April 1978 (RTs also finished on south London routes 54, 89 and 122 on the same day). RT1538 was one of a trio of Regents working the route during the late afternoon and evening (the other two being RTs Nos 785 and 3750). In the upper picture the Regent is waiting in Commonside at Keston, while the crew consult 'possibly' the timetable or maybe even the route map. In the lower picture (ID) RT1538 is setting off back to Bromley, as indicated on the direction sign, with the 16.54 departure. Note the 'last day' yellow slip poster in the passenger window.

RT1538 again, waiting to depart Bromley North with the 15.43 departure to Keston (see previous pictures taken after its arrival on its subsequent short trip). Waiting in front is RM348 on the 119 to Croydon. A modern office complex has since replaced the building in the background.

RT785 was working the next duty that ran through to Downe. It is waiting outside St Mary's Church for its 17.21 departure time back to Bromley. Note the steam being emitted from underneath the radiator. A number of the local residents were well informed and took the opportunity to capture the event on their cameras. The K6-style phone kiosk was still there in 2019 and the Queens Head public house was still dispensing pints of beer.

Above and below: The impromptu notice on the radiator of RT3750 reads 'LAST RT BUS ROUTE 146 21 APRIL 1978'. In the above tranquil view the Regent is about to depart on the penultimate journey to Bromley North at 21.54. While the picture below (taken from the church yard) depicts RT3750, now decked out inside with flags, streamers and balloons, waiting for the final departure time at 22.45. Following the run back to Bromley, RT3750 then did a short working back to Keston with a full standing load. At Keston the landlord of the Fox Inn emerged with a bottle of bubbly and toasted the crew before their very last run (just before midnight). The photographer and his companion then alighted in Westmoreland Road and watched the Regent disappear into the night, heading back to Bromley garage.

Inside RT3750 for its last trip back from Downe. This Regent had arrived at Bromley in March 1975 and continued in service until the 94 was converted to RM-operation in August. From the following day the route was worked by 'OPO' Bristol LH types. An hourly service was still provided in 2019 with the last departure then being at 23.20.

Regents Nos 714, 2146 and 3220 were photographed in Bromley garage yard on Friday 25 August 1978, the penultimate day of RT-operation at both Bromley and Catford garages (on the 94) and indeed of these venerable buses south of the Thames. Only Barking then retained an allocation of the type for routes 62 and 87.

By the following weekend RT3220 had been moved to Dalston garage for Driver Training duties. It is seen on 2 September parked in the entrance to West Ham garage. New in June 1950 it worked as a country bus until June 1967. Following an overhaul it was painted red and started its central area career at Merton. It was last recorded in Spain in 1982.

TL Catford

Overhauling of RTs at Aldenham Works ceased in February 1970 but thereafter a number of the type were recertified at individual garages. Catford garage's long term resident RT3655 is seen in the yard at Camberwell garage on 24 September 1974. Originally a country bus, it moved to the central area at Catford in May 1965 where it stayed until withdrawal in December 1976.

Above and below: Catford garage latterly provided RTs for routes 54, 75 and 94 and continued to turn out odd examples on the 1 and the 47. RT2318 is seen departing Farnborough on the long journey to Shoreditch on 17 July 1977 (above) while earlier in the year RT2788 has just arrived at the terminus, opposite the George and Dragon (below) (ID). The 229 had been extended from Orpington to replace the 51 from 21 May 1977. The pub was closed in 2003 and demolished four years later and the bus stand was done away with and the area landscaped in 1985.

The first new bus station in Lewisham was opened on 22 April 1978 when the bus stands in Molesworth Street and Rennell Street ceased to be used. Catford has turned out RT489 on the 47 on the penultimate day of RT-operation in south London, 25 August 1978, while Bromley's RT4190 has arrived from Orpington on the 94.

The 54 ran from Croydon to Woolwich Arsenal via Elmers End, Catford, Lewisham and Blackheath. On Monday–Friday it was exclusively worked by Catford garage, requiring twenty RTs. On Saturdays RMs were provided from Catford and Elmers End while on Sundays the route was 'OPO' with Fleetlines. RT3853 is seen in Molesworth Street, adjacent to the old Gaumont Palace Theatre, on 7 October 1976.

Above and below: Two views at the Woolwich terminus in General Gordon Square depict RT3840 (above) on 7 October 1976 and RT4448 (below) on 21 April 1978. The imposing building alongside, known as Equitable House, was opened in 1935 and was the home of the Woolwich (Building Society) until 1989. This section of the Square has since been pedestrianised. RT4448 is seen on the last day of RT-operation on the 54 with the route going over to full 'OPO' the following day.

RT2047 was photographed at Blackheath on 31 January 1977. It is seen in Charlton Way, crossing the junction of Maze Hill. In 1166 the common was recorded as Black Heath Field; it is one of the largest protected commons in London and spans 211.5 acres. It is managed by Lewisham and Greenwich councils.

When new in February 1948, RT489 was fitted with a roofbox Weymann-built body. On 1 June 1977 it was captured in Beckenham High Street on a 54 working to Woolwich. In the intervening years it worked from at least nine other garages. In 2019 the premises of Carnation Cleaners was occupied by Allure Home & Gifts.

On Monday–Friday the Croydon layover point of the 54 was in Park Lane. However on Sat/Sun the route terminated at West Croydon Bus Station. RT815 is seen at the bus station on Saturday 16 July 1977. On this day of the week the normal vehicle requirement was for twelve RMs from Catford and three RMs from Elmers End.

RT1088 is seen in Addiscombe Road in Croydon at the junction of Clyde Road on 1 June 1977. This junction was substantially remodelled in the late 1990s with the construction of the Croydon Tramlink (since renamed London Trams), with the only point of reference now being the fence on the right and even that is hidden behind landscaping.

On 10 March 1978 RT2047 is seen in Croydon Road at Elmers End Green heading north to Woolwich. Following the conversion of the route to 'OPO' the following month RT2047 was sent to Walworth for a brief period of Training duties. Ptl Interiors Ltd has since been replaced by Wise Insurance Services Ltd.

RT4625 was captured on the last day of RT-operation on the 54 in Lewisham High Street. This part of the High Street is now known as Lewis Grove and is partly pedestrianised. The 1930s Art Deco Woolworth's building in the background is now occupied by Gap and Superdrug. RT4625 was sold to Wombwell Diesels two months later for scrap.

Route 75 also ran from Croydon to Woolwich and crossed the 54 at Catford before continuing on to Blackheath. RT4285 is seen at the Station Road terminus in West Croydon Bus Station. St Michael's Road, on the left, has since been blocked off and the imposing brick building has been demolished. The east/southbound track of the London Tramway now passes through this exact spot.

RT3202 is seen in Prince Charles Road (partly previously known as Rotten Row) at Blackheath, passing the Andrew Gibb (an Alderman of the Borough of Greenwich who died in 1908) Memorial, on 31 January 1977. RT3202, originally a country bus, was recertified at Aldenham in January 1976 and finished as a PSV at Bromley in June 1978.

Two of Catford's finest, RT Nos 501 and 625 (a former country bus), are also seen in Prince Charles Road on the same day; they are approaching the junction of Prince of Wales Road. At the start of 1977 Catford was still turning out fifty-five Regents on Monday–Friday for routes 54, 75 and 94 although they were replaced on the 75 four weeks after this picture was taken by 'OPO' Fleetlines.

A busy scene in Rennell Street in Lewisham on 7 October 1976 sees two of Catford's Regents on varying route 94 diagrams. While RT4033 would be going no further than Petts Wood, RT4008 would be travelling beyond Orpington and heading back north to Sidcup, with the latter section of route only being covered during Monday–Friday peak hours. Rennell Street, once a comparatively quiet thoroughfare, is now part of the busy A20 as it passes through the centre of Lewisham.

The regular Orpington terminus was situated in St Andrews Drive, a quiet residential street to the northeast of the town centre. RT2730 was recorded on 7 October 1976. Little has changed at this location although it is no longer a bus stand.

The sleek curve of the front end and the classic vertical lines of the rear end are aptly demonstrated on these two Regents that were parked in Lewisham's Rennell Street on 10 March 1978. Both Catford machines, they are RT Nos 1152 and 3513. Both went for scrap a couple of months later.

RT4558 has just left Catford garage (on the right) and is heading north along Bromley Road towards Catford town centre (despite showing Orpington on the blind) on 10 March 1978. Later in the year this Regent was sold to a concern based in (West) Germany.

Earlier in the year, on 21 January 1978, RT3284 is seen making its way down Bromley High Street. It has stopped outside the Abbey National Building Society. Barratts (shoes) and Dixons (electronics) were well-known high street brand names in the 1970s. This section of the High Street is now pedestrianised. The destination of Bromley Common Crown is somewhat interesting as the Crown was one-and-a-half miles north of the garage.

Catford's RT3351 is seen in Queensway at Petts Wood on the penultimate day of RT-operation on the 94. As a sign of the times Warren's Hardware Store had become Refax Vapes by 2019 and Dolland & Aitchison Opticians was a Boots outlet. RT3351 next had a short period as a Trainer at Bow garage before suffering the inevitable fate.

Also at Petts Wood on the same day but seen travelling in the opposite direction along Southborough Road is RT4558. Catford was responsible for providing twelve buses on Monday–Friday on this route while Bromley turned out ten. Twenty-eight years of continuous RT-operation on this route was about to come to an abrupt end – three years longer than the age of this RT.

Ranks of RTs are seen parked up on Catford garage's forecourt on Friday 21 April 1978, the last day of RT-operation on the 54. At the head of each row from the left are RT Nos 840, 579 and 4803, with 579 already having been taken out of service. The AEC badges had probably long since disappeared from the radiators (ID).

CM Chelsham

London Country route 403 ran from West Croydon to Chelsham via Sanderstead and Warlingham and was still being regularly worked by Regents in 1977, despite having first been converted to 'OPO' way back in 1971. RT3461 was one of only three operational RTs painted in NBC colours (at Northfleet with the other two being RT Nos 604 and 1018) and is seen at West Croydon on 1 June 1977. The bus station site was originally the site of the Croydon Canal basin.

RT994 was delivered new to London Country at Northfleet garage in October 1948 and initially worked on routes 487 and 488. After sixteen moves between garages it finally ended its days at Chelsham and is seen in Wellesley Road in the centre of Croydon on 7 October 1976. It was scrapped at C F Booth's yard in Rotherham the following year.

RT2777 was originally a central area red bus and was only painted green in January 1964 when it was allocated to Leatherhead, where it was photographed on 6 December 1976, although by then it was allocated to Chelsham for Training duties. It also passed to Booth's for scrapping in 1977. The backend of on-loan Bournemouth Transport (Yellow Buses) Daimler Fleetline No. 199 has crept onto the left hand side of the picture.

Seen departing the 403 stand at West Croydon Bus Station on 21 February 1976 is RT3424. Partially visible behind is a red RT on the 75 stand. The elevated houses in the background are situated in Oakfield Road. West Croydon Bus Station has been rebuilt on more than one occasion with the latest incarnation having been opened in October 2016. The London Tramway now also runs across the back of the bus station.

RF690 was delivered new to London Country in November 1953 and was one of the last of the type to be built. On 16 July 1977 the veteran Regal, then allocated to Grays and sporting NBC colours, was photographed departing West Croydon Bus Station on the 725 to Windsor, deputising for a Green Line bus. It was withdrawn three months later.

TC Croydon

For many years, after the Second World War, Croydon garage had an all double-deck allocation other than for route 234A. First inaugurated on 3 August 1938 the route was transferred from Sutton to Croydon in April 1944. It ran between Hackbridge and Purley Old Lodge Lane from February 1950 until October 1978 when the northern terminus was cut back to Wallington Station. RF Regal IVs were associated with the route from May 1953 until January 1977, when Bristol LH types took over. On Sunday 5 December 1976 (on which day of the week only two buses were required) the photographer took a ride on RF392, which is first seen at Old Lodge Lane (above) and then at Hackbridge Elm Avenue (below). The building behind the bus in the above view has since been replaced by new houses. The route was withdrawn on 4 February 1984.

DT Dartford

Dartford's last country RF was withdrawn in January 1976 but there still remained a small number of original Green Line vehicles in use, which continued to deputise for other types. On 21 February 1976 RF173 and RF596 were awaiting disposal (above), having been withdrawn in August 1975 and January 1976 respectively; both went to the scrap merchants. On the same day RF221 could be found inside the garage (below). This bus was the last but one green RF to be withdrawn, remaining at Dartford until September 1978 when it was transferred to Chelsham, where it eked out a further two months of service. It was only formally withdrawn in April 1980, following a period of storage.

New in April 1952, RF221 was transferred to Dartford from Chelsham in October 1975. Twelve months later it was photographed in Bromley High Street working on the 725 to Gravesend. The Royal Bell hotel dates from the seventeenth century and was rebuilt in its current form in 1898. It is a Grade II listed building but by 2019 it had fallen out of use and was unoccupied.

AM Plumstead

By 1976 Plumstead garage was responsible for providing buses for just three routes; namely the 99, 122 and 122^{A}, which required just two types of vehicles – DMS Fleetlines and RT Regents. Thirty-three of the latter were required for the Monday–Friday schedules for the 122, which meandered between Crystal Palace and Slade Green via Eltham and Woolwich. RT1328 is seen setting out from Crystal Palace Parade on 9 April 1977.

Sandwiched between an RM and a DMS at Crystal Palace Parade is RT2541, again seen on 9 April 1977. This RT survived until the last day of RT-operation at Barking. Unlike some of the RFs, all of the Regents retained their gold fleet names and numbers to the very end.

RT1703 has paused for a crew change in Wickham Lane at Plumstead on 30 January 1977. Plumstead garage was just to the right of this picture. Opened in October 1913, the garage was closed in October 1981, along with Abbey Wood, with both garages being replaced by a new garage located near Plumstead Station.

Photographed alongside the erstwhile Gaumont Theatre in Molesworth Street in the centre of Lewisham on 2 June 1977 were RT4001 and RM1390. The Regent was withdrawn a few months later and was moved to Harrow Weald for use as a staff bus. The 151 was a very short route that required just two buses Monday–Saturday. Introduced in November 1972 with RTs from New Cross, it was converted to RM-operation in January 1975.

On a bright and crisp day at the end of January 1977 RT2293 was captured in Well Hall Road. It has just crossed Shooters Hill Road and is drawing away from the bus stop near the junction. The same two bus services still served this stop in 2019 – the 122 from Plumstead garage to Crystal Palace and the 161 from North Greenwich to Chislehurst.

Above and below: A bustling street market in Beresford Square at Woolwich is disturbed only by the passage of motor vehicles and these two RTs are picking their way through the crowds of shoppers. Heading west on 9 April 1977 is RT3771 (above) while going in the opposite direction is RT1800 (below). Forty years later this was a much safer place with the square having been pedestrianised. The EWS Butchers had become The Photo Specialists while the, nigh on 200 years old, Ordnance Arms (lower right) had changed its name to O'Connor's. At the time this was the only RT-operated route that regularly passed through Woolwich as the 54, 161, 161^{A} and 229 all terminated there.

RT1989 is seen heading south along Stondon Park at Brockley Rise on 21 January 1978. Having been displaced from Enfield in August 1977 RT1989 worked off Plumstead until April 1978 before being transferred to Barking for further service. The price of petrol was then 75.5 pence per gallon or 16.63 pence per litre, compared to £1.25 per litre in December 2019.

The last day of RT-operation on the 122 was Friday 21 April 1978; RTs also finished on the 54, 89 and 146 on this day. Seen heading east along Broadway at Bexleyheath are RT Nos 1654 and 1791; while the former has terminated at Bexleyheath and is showing the return destination, the latter is working on the 89 to Eltham. The buildings on the far left were occupied by Jennings in the 1950s, an emporium that sold a variety of goods from footwear to toys. The main building was later home to Sainsbury's and latterly SpecSavers.

RT2972 is seen racing alongside the former garrison of the Royal Military Academy (RMA) in Academy Road at Shooters Hill on the last day of RT-operation on the 122. It has left Woolwich behind and is heading towards Eltham. Twelve months as a Trainer was to follow at Bow garage before this Regent was despatched to Yorkshire for scrapping. The RMA, which closed as such in 1939, was superceded by Sandhurst College for the training of all military officers, in 1947.

The lady in the red coat is clearly watching the photographer with a somewhat vacant expression on her face. Perhaps she is more concerned as to what type of bus might appear on the 122 the following day. Meanwhile a group of passengers are boarding RT3365 as it waits in Greens End at Woolwich. The Bond Employment Bureau had become H. & S. Halal Meat Market by 2019.

In answer to the question posed under the previous picture, the following day would see the route operated by Routemasters. In this view RT4566 is leading RT714 along Eltham Road, with the junction of Sidcup Road on the right. The former went on to be the last RT in use as a Training Vehicle with LT, finally being disposed of in April 1980.

LH Leatherhead

By 1976 there were just over forty green RTs still licensed for service with most of these located at garages south of the river. Chelsham had seventeen Regents while Leatherhead was still using seven of the type, mainly on the 406. On 30 March 1979 RT4563 was photographed leaving Leatherhead garage on Driver Training duties. At the time it was allocated to Addlestone, having last been used as a PSV at Windsor in 1976.

Route 418 ran between Kingston Bus Station and Little Bookham. It was normally operated by AEC Swifts from Leatherhead garage. At the start of 1977 there were just three Regals still allocated there for sundry duties, one of which was RF79. Seen on 16 July 1977 it was withdrawn, along with RF54, three months later.

Route 406 ran from Kingston Bus Station to Redhill via Surbiton, Epsom, Tattenham Corner and Tadworth, a distance of around eight miles. RT4344 was the only occupant of Kingston's Wood Street Bus Station when photographed on 7 September 1974; it was withdrawn the following May. Route 406 celebrated its centenary in 2020.

Above and below: Two more of Leatherhead's dwindling stable of Regents were photographed in Kingston on 29 May 1976. RT2157 had Norbiton's RM344 for company at Wood Street (above) while RT3450 is just setting out on a short journey to Tadworth (below). The latter is seen in Richmond Road (later incorporated as part of Clarence Street). On the right two RFs can be seen poking out of Kingston's main bus station. Wood Street Bus Station is thought to have come into being in the mid-1940s. It was used as an overspill parking ground until use of the coal yard was obtained; closure came at the end of 1978. RT2157 outlived Leatherhead's other RTs by nine months, being withdrawn in December 1977.

Also on 29 May 1976 RT3502 was photographed in Richmond Road. It is seen opposite the main bus station while Wood Street Bus Station was just round the corner on the left. The buildings on view have since been demolished and it is no longer possible to drive straight ahead after passing under the railway with a new bridge having been built under the railway leading off Wood Street at the opposite end of the station.

RT4202 is seen among a mixture of bus types in the garage yard at Leatherhead on 9 October 1976. While the Regent would retain LCBS colours to the very end, everything else has been repainted in NBC leaf green. Other than a brief spell at Crawley RT4202 was first allocated to Leatherhead in November 1968 after swapping its Weymann body for a Park Royal version; it was withdrawn in March 1977.

Another picture of RT2157 sees the Regent skirting Epsom Racecourse on Epsom Downs; on the left is the junction of Tattenham Crescent. This wintery scene was recorded on 6 December 1976. On Epsom Derby day a special service 406F was operated to the Downs from Epsom Station. Other than a clutter of road signs this view is unchanged today.

Q Camberwell

RT4118 had last seen PSV use at Bexleyheath in October 1976. Twenty-one months later it was photographed on its then home turf as it passes RM1430 in Camberwell Road. This Regent began life with LCBS in April 1951, working from Hertford garage. The National Westminster Bank, on the corner of Camberwell New Road, had become a doctor's surgery by 2019.

Also allocated to Camberwell at the time for Training duties, but seen resting on South Croydon garage on 15 October 1978, was RT1755. It had latterly been used on the 122 at Plumstead. Former London Country coach-seated Routemaster RCL2234 was working as a Trainer from Abbey Wood at the time, having just been purchased from LCBS.

Merton retained a significant number of RTs for route 155 until it was converted to RM-operation on 9 January 1977. The 155 was the last regularly RT-operated route to venture into central London as it returned by way of Westminster or Blackfriars Bridge and Victoria Embankment during Monday–Friday peak hours. RT2737 is seen in Francis Grove at Wimbledon on 6 December 1976. The only identifying feature of this picture in 2019 was the tree, with all the buildings on view having been replaced with more modern ones.

NB Norbiton

Principally for operational purposes, Kingston's route 215 was supplied by RFs that were maintained at Norbiton garage. These latterly also assisted on the 201 during the week. RF536 is seen between duties in Wood Street on 9 October 1976. A new road has since been constructed that passes under the railway at this location.

The 65 had shed its RTs in favour of RMs on 19 October 1975. However, as the Routemaster shortage began to bite two RTs were sent to Norbition to help out. RT4610 arrived in October but had been sold to Wombwell Diesels by January 1977. RM2100 was part of the usual allocation for the 65 when this picture was taken on 5 December 1976.

AF Putney

In late 1976 Putney garage had a small allocation of RTs to help out on routes 30 and 74. This panned shot sees RT3559 in the gloom, swinging out of Upper Richmond Road into Putney High Street, as it heads for Hackney Wick on 5 December 1976. The Regent's stay at Putney was a brief one as it moved to Turnham Green as a staff bus in March 1977.

RG Reigate

A scene at Wood Street Bus Station in Kingston on 7 September 1974 depicts LT Daimler DMS730 and London Country Regent RT4747. The Fleetline entered service that January and saw less than seven years' use while the Regent put in twenty-three years of hard graft. The 406 was jointly operated by Reigate and Leatherhead garages. By 2019 this former bus station was in use as a taxi rank.

RT981 was allocated to Reigate between November 1976 and February 1978 when it mainly saw use on the 406. Although the route didn't actually pass through Leatherhead RT981 is seen in Bridge Street, returning out of service from the garage on 16 July 1977. The mock Tudor building, seen here occupied by the Woolwich Building Society, was latterly the home of Barton's Bookshop, which regrettably closed in February 2019.

A few weeks earlier, on Epsom Derby Day, RT981 is seen again plying its trade on the 406 as it picks its way along Tattenham Corner Road. An additional special 406F service would normally be run on Derby Day from Epsom Station. Following use as a training vehicle and various periods of storage RT981 was bought for preservation.

SP Sidcup

Sidcup garage was still a prolific user of Regents at the start of 1976, turning out fifty-eight buses on Monday–Friday for routes 51, 51^A, 161, 228 and 229. The first of these to lose its RTs was the 51 on 13 June 1976 when RMs took over. RT2526 is reposing in Orpington High Street on 21 February 1976. Walt Disney's *The Absent Minded Professor* is showing at the EMI (originally the Commodore) cinema. Both the cinema, which was closed in 1982, and the Wimpy Bar have long gone.

The 51 and 51^A followed the same route between Woolwich and Orpington with the former continuing on to Farnborough and the latter to Green Street Green. Also seen in Orpington High Street, but on 7 October 1976, is RT4647. The building behind the bus is part of the Old Village Causeway built during the 1930s. Highsize Fashions latterly became American Golden Nails.

Sidcup provided nine RTs on Monday–Friday for the 161 while the Sunday allocation was also for nine buses, but from March 1975 these had been RMs from both Abbey Wood and Sidcup. RT1303 waits in Powis Street in Woolwich town centre on 7 October 1976. A modern building known as Wick Tower now occupies the space on the right.

On Monday 31 January 1977 RT2676 was photographed crossing Shooters Hill Road as it preceded south from Academy Road into Well Hall Road. The 161 only ran beyond Chislehurst to Sidcup garage during the Monday–Friday peak periods. RT2676 moved to Leyton for the 230 in May 1977 and then to Bexleyheath in January 1978.

RT1341 reposes at the Chislehurst War Memorial terminus on 7 October 1976; the setting hasn't changed in over forty years since this picture was taken. The autumnal sun casts shadows of the tree foliage over the bus as the crew chat in the lower-deck saloon before their return departure to Woolwich.

Sidcup also provided buses for the 228 that ran from Eltham Well Hall to Chislehurst via Sidcup; again nine Regents were rostered on Monday–Friday. The Chislehurst terminus was alongside the Gordon Arms in Alexander Road where RT2029 was photographed on 7 October 1976. The Belmont Cafe is now simply called the Belmont, but is now a dry cleaning establishment. The 228 was withdrawn in 1986, rendering the stand obsolete.

Above and below: The old Well Hall Bus Station at Eltham was on the opposite side of Well Hall Road to the new bus station, which was built in conjunction with the upgrading of the A2 trunk road. These two views, taken on 7 October 1976, show RT1138 (above) and RT4426 (below) on the 228 with Fleetline DMS201 on the 132 to Slade Green Station. RTs were removed from the 228 from 21 May 1977 when RMs took over the Monday–Saturday duties. RT1138 was exported to France while RT4426 saw further PSV use at Harrow Weald.

The 229 ran from Woolwich to Orpington Station and was shared between Bexleyheath and Sidcup garages. Sidcup's RT1892 is seen in Orpington High Street on 21 February 1976 on the last leg of its journey to the station. The Gas Showroom is now shared by Rymans and SpecSavers.

Sidcup garage remained an RT-stronghold until 21 May 1977 when routes 51A, 161, 228 and 229 all lost the type at the same time – more than forty RTs were made redundant in one fell swoop. Only a couple of months before the cull, RT Nos 4020 and 924 are seen on the garage forecourt. While RT924 moved to Harrow Weald, RT4020 was made redundant. Back in the 1950s Sidcup had virtually an all-Leyland RTL allocation; it was closed in 1988 (ID).

SW Stockwell

RT1599 was destined for fame and longevity. It was selected to lead the Silver Jubilee SRM cavalcade from South Carriage Drive at Hyde Park on 10 April 1977. Earlier that day, and having been specially repainted, it is seen at Stockwell garage in the company of two other parade participants – namely RML2661 and former Midland Red BMMO D9 No. OM4. After further PSV service at Harrow Weald and Bromley (see pp. 22–3) it was bought for preservation.

AK Streatham

RT2629 had last seen service as a PSV working from Walworth garage on the 176 and 176^{A}, which were converted to RM-operation in March 1976. After a short period of store at Bexleyheath it was transferred to Streatham for Training duties, in September 1976. Looking quite pristine it is seen just weeks later in Crystal Palace Parade on 7 October.

A Sutton

On Sunday 5 December 1976 a visitor to Sutton garage would have been confronted by this line-up. From the left they are RT Nos 2623, 1791, 3389, 3986 and RM Nos 1571 and 1283. The 93 had been converted to RM-operation back in March but Regents were still rostered for the 164 and 164^{A}.

The following day RT2212 was observed heading north on the 93 and is seen at Wimbledon Broadway. The route terminated just beyond the north bank of the Thames. The building behind was the old Wimbledon Town Hall, which ceased to function as such when the Borough of Wimbledon was abolished in 1965.

Routes 164 and 164A both started outside Morden LT Tube Station and ran south to Banstead where they diverged – the 164 continuing to Epsom and the 164A to Tattenham Corner. On 6 December 1976 RT4004 was photographed in Epsom High Street on the 164. A lone figure can be seen eyeing up the merchandise in a shop window – in 2019 this shop was Cabello Hair & Beauty Salon while a TK Maxx store had been built on the vacant plot behind the bus.

RTs were introduced to the 164 and 164A in 1953 and remained the scheduled type exclusively from the following year until October 1976 when RMs took over on Sundays. Meanwhile the Regents gained a short reprieve and continued in use Monday–Saturday until 15 January 1977. RT525 is seen at the Tattenham Corner terminus on 6 December 1976.

To quote a famous line from the film *The Full Monty*, 'And For One Night Only', although in this case read 'For One Day Only', RTs were reintroduced to route 164^A on Wednesday 1 June 1977 to convey race goers from Morden Station to Tattenham Corner for the Epsom Derby. The buses used were recently refurbished examples and RT2177, which was allocated to Bromley and had also received a full repaint, was recorded in Sutton Lane at Banstead on its journey south. This Regent survived into preservation.

RT4053 had recently been recertified at Walworth garage and was frequently turning out on the 12 when it was given a day off to supplement the 164^A. It is seen at Tattenham Corner with the Beefeater pub on the right.

RT3365 is seen at Tattenham Corner and is already showing a return destination of St Helier, a district of Morden. RT3365 had been recertified in May 1975 and had been a Sutton allocated bus. However by this date it was working off Plumstead on the 122. It passed to the Giraffe Bus Co. in Lusaka, Zambia in July 1979.

SJ Swanley

RF134 was allocated to Swanley garage when it was photographed in the centre of Dartford on 21 February 1976 on local route 400. It was withdrawn three months later and sold to Booth's at Rotherham. Hall-Thermotank Ltd was formed in 1959 (originally established in 1785 by smithy and millwright John Hall) following a merger of two companies. A manufacturer of refrigeration and air conditioning equipment, the company has passed through several takeovers but still existed in 2019, although by then in Japanese ownership. There is no longer a factory in Dartford.

WD Wandsworth

RT837 was one of two Regents allocated to Wandsworth (on the south bank of the river) in the latter part of 1976 to help out on the 28. It is seen with non-standard blinds in West End Lane at West Hampstead on 26 March 1977. The Chinese restaurant was serving Japanese cuisine in 2019.

WR Windsor

RF125 had a long and varied career working as a Green Line RF, beginning at Hemel Hempstead garage in February 1952. It was one of the last handful of the type still in service with London Country and is seen here in Bromley Market Square on 16 July 1977. Latterly allocated to Windsor in January 1977 it managed twelve months service from that garage before final withdrawal exactly a year later.

NF Northfleet

RFs continued to make appearances on the 725 for as long as they remained in service. On 4 December 1976 RF202 was recorded proceeding down Staines High Street and was allocated to Northfleet garage at the time. With the last of the red RFs having been withdrawn at the end of March 1979, RF202 was the very last Regal to see service in the metropolis, not being withdrawn by London Country until July 1979. It is now preserved.

WL Walworth

Rush hour on Monday 6 December 1976 and RT3513 is stuck in traffic at the Elephant & Castle. Some passengers have decided to alight into the roadway despite the obstacle of a pedestrian guardrail. First allocated there in 1966, RT3513 was still working from Walworth some nine months after RTs had been removed from the 176 and 176A.

K Kingston

Route 71 ran from Richmond (Dee Road) to Leatherhead LCBS garage and required fourteen RTs on Monday–Friday. In a setting that was largely unchanged more than forty years later, RT4286 was photographed passing Richmond Station on 26 March 1977. Kingston was the last garage that RT4286 worked from as a PSV.

In this view RT1207 has just crossed Richmond Road at Ham on Saturday 16 July 1977 and is passing a modern-day brick sculpture as it proceeds down Tudor Drive. Only eight buses were required to operate the route on a Saturday. RT1207 was sold to Wombwell Diesels for scrap just two months later.

RT2816 is seen drifting down Petersham Road as it leaves Richmond behind on 16 July 1977; it is passing the junction of Compass Hill. On the left is Belle Vue House, a Georgian detached house that dates from the late eighteenth century and which when built would have had an elevated unobstructed view (from the back) of the River Thames.

With the introduction of a new one-way system in the centre of Kingston in July 1963 buses travelled south to north via Wood Street. In this view RT1107 is seen picking up passengers in Wood Street adjacent to the bus/railway station on 16 July 1977. This section of Wood Street was originally known as Ceres Road. Nothing in this view now exists as redevelopment has seen a total transformation of the area.

Above and below: On this page are two pictures of Regents traversing Leatherhead Road, near the Fox and Hounds (since renamed the Shy Horse) at Chessington, on 16 July 1977. In the upper picture RT1049 is not ploughing a furrow through the field but is travelling south on the tarmac road surface. In the lower picture RT734 is heading north and has just passed the junction of Rushett Lane (although the Richmond terminus was in Dee Road the blind is showing Lower Mortlake Road). The 71 managed to hang on to its Regents until 3 March 1978; thereafter Routemasters were in charge Monday–Saturday with Bristol LHs having replaced the RFs on Sundays from 26 September 1976. RT1049 (originally a country area bus) was sent to the breaker's yard the following month while RT734 suffered the same fate in February 1978.

RT734 is seen again in Richmond Road (now part of Clarence Street with the direction of travel reversed) in the centre of Kingston on 29 May 1976. It is on a short working to the Ham Estate (Ashburnham Road); RF527 is following close behind. Virtually all the buildings in this view have since been demolished.

At the beginning of 1976 Kingston's vehicle allocation still included a number of RTs for route 71 for operation Monday–Saturday (RFs were scheduled on Sunday). Such were the cramped conditions at this old garage that the Regents would normally be parked up in the coal yard opposite the garage. RT4154 is seen in Guildford Road on 6 December 1976 approaching journey's end at Leatherhead garage.

Above and below: At the beginning of 1976 Kingston garage had a stable of around forty RFs (sixty-three different examples were associated with the garage during the 1970s) for routes 201/15/16/18/19 while a further nine were out based at nearby Norbiton to supplement the 201 and 215. One of the latter's allocation RF330, with RF404 lurking in the background (above), is seen in Kingston Bus Station waiting to depart for Church Cobham on 29 May 1976. On the same day RF371 (below) was waiting to depart for Staines via Sunbury Village on the 216. Both these routes were converted to Bristol LH operation later in the year; the 215 on 24 October and the 216 on 26 September. Both of these Regals were bought by private owners but there is no reference to either after 1980.

Kingston was unusual in that the bus station and garage were part of the same complex and that buses entered the bus station through the garage entrance in Cromwell Road. Having said that, the bus station was opened six years after the garage, in 1928. Alas this classic structure (latterly used by Westlink in the 1990s) was demolished in the early 2000s to make way for the Rotunda Complex. A new bus station had already been opened on the site of the old Cromwell Road coal yard on 15 July 1995. Taking shelter under the canopy on 29 May 1976 were home-based RT4286 and RF390.

Another scene captured in Richmond Road on the same day. The 65 was worked by Norbiton garage (except Sundays) and had retained RT-operation until 19 October 1975. RM336 has just terminated at Kingston with a journey from the north (most probably from Ealing Broadway). Meanwhile RF412 has just left the bus station (centre distance) on a 219 journey to Weybridge Station. This locality is now almost unrecognisable.

The 201 was a short route that ran from Kingston to Hampton Court and that, from April 1976, had a three-garage involvement. On a Saturday the four buses required were split evenly between Kingston and Fulwell garages while on Monday–Friday Norbiton provided three buses in lieu of Fulwell's two. An empty RF444 is seen in Wood Street (née Ceres Road) in Kingston on 29 May 1976. The 201 went over to Bristol LHs in November of that year.

RFs were first introduced as crewed buses to routes 218 and 219 in February 1960. They were converted to 'OPO' in September 1968. The two services followed the same route as far as Hersham and the buses were interworked between the two. On Saturday 4 December 1976 RF425 was photographed in Heath Road at Weybridge with just a short distance to go to the British Aircraft Corporation (BAC) Works.

Above and below: Route 218 ran from Kingston to Staines via Esher, Hersham, Walton-on-Thames, Shepperton and Laleham with a running time of just over an hour. Two pictures taken on 4 December 1976 depict RF534 in Clarence Street in Staines town centre (above) and RF489 at the terminus in Staines (below). Behind the buses is what used to be the main frontage building of Staines West Railway Station (terminus). It was opened on 2 November 1885 by the London & South Western Railway and closed by British Rail on 29 March 1965. Although this locality is no longer used as a bus terminal and has since been landscaped the station building was still in use in 2019 and occupied by Orchid Design & Marketing Ltd. AEC Swift SMD52 can be seen on the right on a route 90 working for Richmond.

Another view at the Staines terminus, taken in October 1977, sees RF485 in the company of two Routemasters. The Regal was withdrawn three months later while the 117 was converted to 'OPO' with Leyland Nationals around the same time. RM583 was allocated to Hounslow at the time and was recorded as being with the West Coast Bus Co. in Vancouver in 2011 (ID).

An unusual view of Regals RF471 and RF507, looking out on to Richmond Road, with RT4286 (again) just visible on the extreme left. While seen here in October 1977 both of these buses survived until the final day of RF-operation. The higgledy-piggledy row of shops across the road have all since been demolished and the soulless brick edifice that was built in their place no longer faces Kingston's 1928 classic bus station (ID).

RF471 and RF502 were caught taking a breather in Esher Road at Hersham in this October 1977 view. This picture could be repeated in 2019 but the buses would most likely be Wrightbus Streetlites operated by Hallmark Buses on their 458 service, which still connected the same places as the erstwhile 218 (ID).

On the same day RF421 was photographed turning out of Hersham Road into Molesley Road with an eastbound working to Kingston. Molesley Road was where the 218 and 219 routes diverged for Staines and Weybridge respectively. RF421 was withdrawn just a couple of weeks after this picture was taken but was saved for preservation (ID).

Above and below: RF471 and RF510 are seen together at Hersham Green on 22 April 1978, both having worked short journeys from Kingston on the 219. Both of these buses gained the LT roundel in lieu of the gold London Transport fleet name. The bus stop and the Waterman Arms are still there but the building on the right has been replaced by a more modern structure, as has the bus shelter that is now served by routes 555 and 564.

Also on 22 April 1978 RF495 was photographed at the Barley Mow bus stop in Esher Road at Hersham. This was the first stop after the 218 and 219 merged to take the same route onwards to Kingston. RF495 was delivered new to Sidcup for the 228 in March 1953. It was modified for 'OPO' in March 1965 and was then allocated to Barking to work the 291. A move to Kingston took place in March 1972 where it stayed until the end of RF operation.

Another period view of the centre of Kingston sees RF369 in Eden Street on 9 December 1978. Behind the Regal is Gough House, which as this book was being compiled was under the threat of demolition for redevelopment. Once a common London high street name, the Brook Street Bureau is now Phone Globe while the bus stop was renumbered to E2.

RF471 again, also on the 9 December 1978, is bound for Staines in this view taken in Walton-on-Thames High Street. Dorothy Perkins was founded in 1909; it was purchased by the Arcadia Group in 1979. The mock Tudor building was demolished to form an entrance to the new Heart Shopping Centre opened in 2006.

The first of a series of pictures taken on the last day of RF-operation, 30 March 1979, depicts RF492 having just arrived at Weybridge Station. The last day was a mainly dry day but dull throughout. RF492 survived for a while after LT use with the King's Royal Rifle Corps at Farnborough but eventually met its end when it was sold for scrap in 1995.

More than likely oblivious to the fact they would never board an RF again, a healthy load of passengers scramble aboard RF502 in Staines High Street. This section of road has since been pedestrianised while the Waitrose building has been refurbished and is now occupied by Bonmarché.

RF520 reposes at the Staines terminus on the final day. As previously recounted this was originally the frontage of Staines West Railway Station. RF520 was one of many of the type that ended its days at Booth's Rotherham scrapyard.

Above and below: In order to serve Walton-on-Thames Railway Station buses on the 218 did a short double-run along Station Avenue from the junction of Hersham Road. Again seen on the last day RF437 (above) waits at bus stop C on its way back to Kingston while RF428 (below), having turned round, is waiting on the opposite side of the road at bus stop D. The lady in the brown coat seems to lack interest in the Regal and the photographer. The British Rail sign (double-arrow logo) was originally known as 'The Arrows of Indecision' and was conceived by the Design Research Unit at Derby in 1964. It is still used to this day on Department of Transport road direction signs and as a general indication of the locations of the UK network's railway stations. These were two more RFs that went directly for scrap.

Above and below: RF507 formed the last journey through to Weybridge BAC Works at 17.53 and after arriving back at Kingston it was scheduled to operate the last 218 journey through to Staines at 21.53, which departed back from Staines at 23.18. The demand for the final out-and-back run required the provision of two duplicates that were provided by RF314 and RF492. In the picture above RF492 has arrived back at Kingston while behind is RF516, which was on the last short working to Walton. Below, RF507 is slowly eased into Kingston garage after arriving back a little after midnight with the last working from Staines.

Disposal

Above and below: In their twilight years the vast majority of redundant RTs were bought by Wombwell Diesels who were located in the Yorkshire town of the same name. Withdrawn Regents were arriving thick and fast during the last few years of their operating careers. The next five pictures were taken on a visit to their final resting place on 23 May 1978. RT2946 (above) ended its days at Seven Kings and first went to Wombwell in August 1977. It then made an appearance on Spike Milligan's *Q7* TV programme in January 1978 before returning to the scrapyard. RT3343 (below) had only arrived that month having also ended its PSV days as a Seven Kings bus.

Above and below: The scrapyard basically consisted of not much more than a large field that in places was badly churned up as a result of the constant moving of buses around the site and the frequent inclement weather that prevailed in that part of the country. However on this day the sun shone on the photographer's visit when these two line-ups were captured. Above: from the left are RT Nos 3982, 4614, 2028 and 915. Below: RT Nos 1087, 1312, 4422 and 3764. Both RT1087 and RT4614 hadn't seen any PSV use since 1969, having been used as a Driver Trainer and as a staff bus respectively. By 1978 Wombwell Diesels was also purchasing redundant DMS Daimler Fleetlines and SMS AEC Swifts from London Transport. In the upper picture an RF and a Swift can just be glimpsed on the extreme right.

Finally on 23 May we see RT4297 looking somewhat forlorn on its own. First allocated to Willesden garage in June 1953, RT4297 then moved successively to Victoria, Forest Gate, Bexleyheath, Wood Green, Poplar, Abbey Wood and then to Brixton, in December 1968, where it remained until February 1976 before taking up its final duties at Walthamstow. After a short spell as a staff bus at Aldenham it was sold to Wombwell in March 1978.

A subsequent visit was made to Wombwell Diesels on 10 September 1979, some five months after the last Regents had run in the Capital. RT4201, on the right, had last worked as a PSV from New Cross in 1973; it then flirted between periods of storage and use as a staff bus until March 1979. RT1654, on the left, was withdrawn from Barking in March 1979.

Three more Regents are seen on 10 September 1979 in an advanced state of dismantling. From the left they are RT Nos 4672, 4559 and 1987. The disastrous Swifts were beginning to arrive in ever increasing numbers. After forty years of trading Wombwell Diesels sold this site in 2005 for redevelopment; new housing now occupies this hallowed ground.

The other main recipient of redundant London buses, particularly RFs, was the South Yorkshire dealer of C. F. Booth, whose yard was situated behind Rotherham United's old Millmoor Football Ground. RF440, which last operated from Kingston garage in December 1976, is seen in a somewhat elevated position on 26 April 1977.

Above and below: Wombwell Diesels was also the final resting place for a number of RFs. In the picture below the line-up consists of (from right to left) RF Nos 513, 617, 334, 519, 432, 448, 387 and 685 (the above picture is a close-up of the last two). Although this picture dates from 23 May 1978, other than RF334 this tranche of Regals was withdrawn from either Hounslow or Kingston garages between January and August 1977, passing to WD in August of that year; so they would have been languishing on the site for a good many months. The odd one out is RF334, which was last used as a PSV at Sutton garage in October 1973 after which it alternated over the next four years between periods of storage and use as a staff bus.

Continental Pioneer was a small independent operator that worked route 235 between Richmond Station and Richmond Hill. However the expansive depot yard was also home to many preserved/privately owned buses. Representing both of London Transport's divisions are RF644 and RF518, both of which are still in existence. This picture was taken on 9 February 1980.

The first picture in this volume was of RT196 in its London Transport days. Here it is again in the yard of Continental Pioneer at Richmond facing former Preston Borough Transport PD3 Rebuild No. 2, on 9 February 1980. Continental Pioneer vacated this yard, adjacent to the railway, in 1985 and the site is now occupied by residential housing.